CCSS Genre Realistic F

Essential Question
How do writers look at success in different ways?

Try, Try Again

by Paul Mason
illustrated by
Juan Caminador

Chapter 1
The New Bike

A week had passed since Jerome's birthday, and he still hadn't ridden his new bike. His older brother Louis found it in a corner of the garage with the bow still **dangling** from the handlebars.

Louis found Jerome lying on his bed surrounded by comics.

"What's up?" Jerome asked.

"You haven't ridden your bike yet," Louis said.

Jerome sighed, "What's the point if I don't know how to ride it?"

"The point is you *learn*," Louis laughed. "You've heard that word before?"

"Very funny," Jerome said.

"Seriously, I can teach you. We can work on it together since Mom and Dad are so busy."

Jerome thought for a moment. "I have been feeling bad that I can't ride my bike," he admitted. "Okay, when do we start?"

"How about right now?" asked Louis.

Louis wheeled the bike out onto the long driveway.

He looked around the yard while Jerome **strapped** on his helmet. There was plenty of space for Jerome to learn, as long as he stayed away from the flower beds.

STOP AND CHECK

Why hasn't Jerome ridden his new bike?

Chapter 2

Lesson Over

Louis held the bike steady while Jerome sat on the seat.

"Here's what we'll do," Louis said. "I'll give you a push. Then hold on and keep steady. Then start pedaling."

Jerome raised his eyebrows. "Are you sure?"

"You'll be fine!" said Louis. "Are you ready?"

Jerome looked worried. "I guess so," he said, gripping the handlebars.

Louis held onto Jerome's shoulder. Louis started pushing, and Jerome gathered speed. With a grunt, Louis gave his brother a shove, sending him racing down the driveway.

Jerome's arms wobbled from side to side. The handlebars wobbled, the bike wobbled, and then he lost control. Thump! Jerome fell off the bike. He **sprawled** onto the grass, his arms outstretched.

Jerome picked himself up. He rubbed his elbow.

"That was your great plan?" he asked angrily.

Louis felt guilty. "Sorry. That wasn't supposed to happen."

"No, it wasn't," Jerome grumbled. "This lesson is over!"

Louis picked the bike up. "It wasn't a good idea to **launch**, or start you off, like that," he admitted, "but we can try again."

Jerome glared at him. "Maybe tomorrow," he said half-heartedly.

STOP AND CHECK

Why does Jerome glare at his brother?

Chapter 3
Learning to Ride

After school the next day, Louis and Jerome took the bike out again. This time Louis stayed close to Jerome, **hovering** behind him. He was ready to catch him if he fell.

Louis taught Jerome how to keep his **balance** so he wouldn't wobble and fall off. He taught him how to use the brakes and how to come to a stop.

They practiced all week. Little by little, Jerome's **confidence** grew as he learned to pedal and steer at the same time. He started to believe he could do it.

STOP AND CHECK

Why is Jerome's confidence growing?

"I want to ride on my own," Jerome said one day. "No shoving this time."

"Sure," said Louis, "if you think you're ready." He stood back and watched as Jerome set off, shakily at first. Jerome slowly gathered speed and pedaled along the driveway.

Jerome reached the end of the driveway. "I'm going to turn around," he called.

But when he tried to turn, he lost his balance and fell into a heap on the grass.

Louis ran over to him. "Are you okay?" he asked.

Jerome laughed, "I'm fine. I rode all by myself!" He stood up and brushed himself off.

Louis beamed. He was really proud of his brother. Jerome had kept trying to **attain** his goal of riding the bike even though he'd had some falls and **tumbles**.

"I think you're ready to show Mom and Dad," said Louis.

STOP AND CHECK

Why is Jerome pleased with himself?

Chapter 4
Triumph

Jerome kept practicing while Louis set up two chairs in the yard. Then Louis went to get their parents. Jerome hid in the garage. His helmet was on, and he was ready to ride.

"What's the big surprise?" asked their mom, with a **suspicious** look on her face.

"You'll see," said Louis.

Louis raised his hand, which was the signal for Jerome to start pedaling. Mom and Dad turned to see Jerome wobbling his way out of the garage. Along the driveway he went, his hands locked onto the handlebars. His legs pedaled quickly.

"Way to go, Jerome!" his mom called.

Jerome reached the end of the driveway. Then he turned around and came back. He even **managed** to raise his hand and wave.

Jerome braked and came to a stop. "Ta-daaa!" he said, raising his arms in **triumph**.

"What a surprise!" said his dad. "When did you learn how to ride, Jerome?"

"Louis taught me," he said, smiling.

"Jerome kept practicing, even though it was hard," said Louis.

"Well," said his mom, "like I always say, if at first you don't succeed. . . ."

"Try, try again," Jerome finished.

STOP AND CHECK

What does Jerome do to show he has learned how to ride the bike?

Respond to Reading

Summarize the important details in *Try, Try Again*. Your graphic organizer may help.

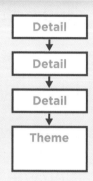

Text Evidence

1. What does Jerome achieve in the story? THEME

2. Find the word *wobbled* on page 6. What does it mean? What clues help you figure it out? VOCABULARY

3. Write about how Jerome became successful at riding his bike. Use details from the story in your answer. WRITE ABOUT READING

Compare Texts

Read about a person who remembers what it was like to learn how to ride a bike.

Sunlight Sparkling on Chrome

Like a river, the path ran before her;
To ride it, she'd made up her mind.
Brave wheels went around and around,
Leaving her home behind.

Never before had she been this far,
To ride so steady, so right.
Brave wheels went around and around;
The handlebars were held tight.

She remembered the falls, the scratches,
Medals of her labor to learn.
Brave wheels went around and around,
Falling no more a concern.

Now she felt soft wind greet her,
A smiling song on her face.
Brave wheels went around and around,
As though she were first in a race.

Sweet rhythm of pedals spinning,
Warm whir of rubber on road.
Brave wheels went around and around,
At last, at the end she slowed.

With a glad sigh, she turned back
And guided her steed for home.
Brave wheels went around and around,
Sunlight sparkling on chrome.

Make Connections

How does the descriptive language help you to understand how the girl feels in *Sunlight Sparkling on Chrome*? ESSENTIAL QUESTION

How do Jerome in *Try, Try Again* and the girl in *Sunlight Sparkling on Chrome* reach their goals? TEXT TO TEXT

Focus on Literary Elements

Repetition Repeating a word or phrase makes readers slow down and take notice. Repetition can help readers focus on the meaning of the words. Repetition also creates a rhythm that can match the meaning of the words, actions, or feelings the poet is expressing.

Read and Find In *Sunlight Sparkling on Chrome*, the repetition of the line "Brave wheels went around and around" helps us understand what the rider feels. The poet uses these words to show that the rider feels brave. When read aloud, the repeated line gives a sense of the bicycle wheels moving. The rhythm and rhyme of each verse also give a sense of the bicycle wheels moving.

Your Turn

In a group, read the poem aloud several times until you can feel the rhythm of the words. Think about how you could perform the repeated line. Will you read it together? Add some movements that go with the poem. Perform your poem for another group.